FOOD & FEASTS

with the

Vikings

Hazel Mary Martell

new Discovery BOOKS

Parsippany, New Jersey

First American publication 1995 by New Discovery Books, an imprint of Silver Burdett Press.
A Simon & Schuster Company
299 Jefferson Road, Parsippany, NJ 07054

First published in 1995 in Great Britain by
Wayland (Publishers) Ltd

A ZOË BOOK

Copyright © 1995 Zoë Books Limited

Devised and produced by
Zoë Books Limited
15 Worthy Lane
Winchester
Hampshire SO23 7AB
England

Printed in Italy by Grafedit SpA.
Design: Jan Sterling, Sterling Associates
Picture research: Victoria Sturgess
Maps: Gecko Limited
Production: Grahame Griffiths

10 9 8 7 6 5 4 3 2 1

Library of Congress Cataloging-in-Publication Data

Martell, Hazel.
  Food & feasts with the Vikings / Hazel Mary Martell.
    p. cm. — (Food & feasts)
  Includes bibliographical references and index.
  ISBN 0-02-726317-7
  1. Vikings—Food—Juvenile literature. 2. Vikings—Social life and customs—Juvenile literature. 3. Northmen—Food—Juvenile literature. 4. Northmen—Social life and customs—Juvenile literature. [1. Food habits—Scandinavia. 2. Vikings—Social life and customs. 3. Cookery, Scandinavian.] I. Title. II. Title: Food and feasts with the Vikings. III. Series.
  DL65.M359 1995
  394.1'2'0948—dc20   94-5429

  Summary: A social history of the Viking peoples in Europe, explaining what foods were eaten and how they were prepared or cooked. Includes information about events that brought about special celebrations and feasts.

Photographic acknowledgments

The publishers wish to acknowledge, with thanks, the following photographic sources:

Antikvarisk - topografiska arkivet, Stockholm 3, 4, 13t, 14t&b, 17br, 23tl, 24l; Archäologisches Landesmuseum, Schloss Gottorf 13br; Arnamagnaean Institute, Reykjavik 10b; British Library, London 10t, 19b; C. M. Dixon 5t, 9t&b, 11t, 12b, 13bl, 15t, 20t&b, 21b; Robert Harding Picture Library / Matyn Chillmaid 6t, / Richard Elliott 7t; Michael Holford 8t, 21t, 24r; Kulturen, Lund 6b, 18b; Nationalmuseet, Copenhagen 12t, 25b; Trondheim University 11b; University of Oslo 7b, 17t, 23tr&b, 25t; University Library, Utrecht 5b; York Archaeological Trust Picture Library title page, 8b, 15b, 16t&b, 17bl, 18t, 19t.

Cover: C. M. Dixon top right; Michael Holford top left; Nationalmuseet, Copenhagen bottom left; University of Oslo bottom right; York Archaeological Trust Picture Library center.

The publishers have made every effort to trace the copyright holders, but if they have inadvertently overlooked any, they will be pleased to make the necessary arrangement at the first opportunity.

Contents

4

Introduction

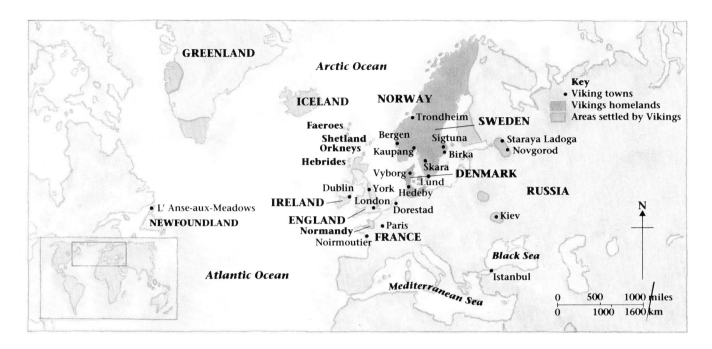

The map labels:

GREENLAND

Arctic Ocean

ICELAND NORWAY

Faeroes
Shetland Bergen Sigtuna SWEDEN
Orkneys Kaupang Birka • Staraya Ladoga
Hebrides Skara • Novgorod
Vyborg DENMARK
Dublin York Lund
IRELAND London Hedeby RUSSIA
• L' Anse-aux-Meadows Dorestad
NEWFOUNDLAND ENGLAND • Kiev
Normandy • Paris
Noirmoutier FRANCE

Trondheim

Black Sea
Istanbul

Atlantic Ocean

Mediterranean Sea

Key
• Viking towns
Vikings homelands
Areas settled by Vikings

N

0 500 1000 miles
0 1000 1600 km

△ The Viking Age lasted about 300 years. This map shows the Vikings' homelands and the places where they settled during that time.

▽ Wood carvings give us a good idea of what the Vikings looked like. This head of a Viking warrior comes from Sigtuna in Sweden.

The Vikings came from the lands we call Denmark, Norway, and Sweden. Their **ancestors** lived by farming. About 1,200 years ago, however, the population began to increase and by the 790s there was not enough good farmland to grow food for everybody.

Some Vikings then looked for new ways to make a living. They were adventurous by nature and, as most of them lived by the sea, they were also excellent shipbuilders. Their **longships** could be sailed or rowed in shallow water as well as on the open sea. Many Vikings set out to find new lands overseas.

The earliest Viking adventurers were robbers, or raiders, who attacked **monasteries** on the coast of England. Their first recorded raid was on the monastery at Lindisfarne in 793. Many more raids followed, not only in England but also in Ireland, Scotland, Wales, the Netherlands, France, Germany, Spain, and Italy. At that time, very few people except **monks** could read or write. Naturally, the

The Viking alphabet was called the futhark after the first six letters in it (*th* counted as one letter). There were only 16 letters altogether. The language was difficult to read as well as to write, because there was not a letter for every sound in the language.

△ The Viking runes on this stone say, "Estrid had this stone erected in memory of Osten, her husband, who went to Jerusalem and died in Greece."

monks did not have anything good to say about the Vikings.

Now, however, **archaeologists** have found evidence to show that the Vikings were not just violent raiders. Many Vikings traveled long distances, buying and selling goods such as silk and jewelry. They were traders. Others settled as farmers in places where they had earlier raided or traded. Some Vikings sailed to Iceland and Greenland. Others visited North America, but their attempts to settle there failed.

Reading and writing were difficult for the Vikings. Their alphabet was made up of sticklike letters called **runes** that could be carved onto stone, metal, or wood. This took a long time and written information was not easy to carry around. Most information was passed on by word of mouth. The Viking adventure stories, or **sagas**, that were written down in the 13th century tell us about Viking feasts. However, no Viking recipes have survived. Almost everything we know about Viking food comes from archaeological evidence.

"The Vikings laid everything to waste. They trampled the holy places with dirty feet, dug up the altars and seized all the treasures of the holy church. They killed some of the brothers. Some they took away with them in chains. Many they drove out, naked and loaded with insults, and some they drowned in the sea."

Simeon of Durham's description of the Viking raid on Lindisfarne in A.D. 793

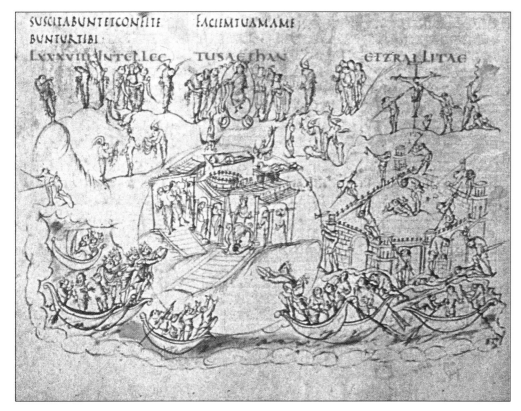

◁ This picture was drawn by a monk in a book called the *Utrecht Psalter*. It shows his idea of a Viking attack on a city in Europe.

Farming and food in the countryside

▷ In Norway, Denmark, and Sweden, most Viking farms were on land that is still used for farming. In Iceland, however, some farms were abandoned in Viking times and never lived in again.

Archaeologists have dug out, or **excavated**, the site of one farm at Stong. The longhouse has been reconstructed from the evidence they found there. Wood was scarce in Iceland, so the house was built from blocks of grass and earth, known as turf.

A Viking farm

Most Vikings lived on farms in the countryside. They had to grow or make everything they needed, including food for their animals, so they spent a lot of time working on their land.

Cheese, milk, and other **dairy produce** played a large part in the Vikings' diet. All farmers kept cattle, and most of them also kept pigs, sheep, goats, hens, and geese for food. When the animals had been killed for their meat, their skins were treated, or tanned, into leather for clothes and household goods. Sheep's wool was spun and woven into cloth, while the feathers from the geese and hens were used to stuff pillows and mattresses.

The main building on the farm was the **longhouse**, where the family lived. It was usually built of wood and had a roof that was **thatched** with straw or reeds. There was a barn, or byre, to shelter the animals in the hard winters. Iron tools

▽ Most of the equipment used in Viking dairies, like this cheese drainer, was made from wood.

▷ As in Viking times, Norwegians today farm along the shores of the inlets, or fjords.

Viking society was divided into three groups—jarls, karls, and thralls. Jarls were wealthy landowners and usually had a lot of power. Karls were also quite wealthy and often owned their own farms. If they had no land, they could work for a friend or relation and still be a free man. Thralls were slaves who had no rights, but they could earn their freedom if they worked hard. If a karl became very poor, he could become a thrall to make sure he had at least food and shelter until the time when he could buy back his freedom.

were made or mended in the **smithy**. If the farmer owned a longship or other boat, there might be a boat shed to keep it in.

Around the longhouse was a garden where the Vikings grew vegetables such as cabbages, leeks, carrots, peas, and beans. They often grew herbs such as mustard, horseradish, and mint to add flavor to their food. There was probably a small orchard with apple trees and plum trees. Beyond the garden were the fields in which barley, oats, wheat, or rye—the **cereal crops**— were grown. These fields were sometimes surrounded by stone walls to stop the animals from trampling the crops. There were also meadows in which grass was grown. It was cut and dried for hay to feed the animals in winter. The work on the farm was usually done by the family, but on the larger farms there were probably also slaves, known as thralls. They helped with the heavy and unpleasant jobs, such as spreading **manure** on the fields in the early spring.

◁ Many Viking farmers made their own tools from iron and wood. They cut the grain crops with **sickles**. The grass for hay was cut with a **scythe**. Tools like these were still being used on farms at the beginning of the 20th century.

The farming year

△ This plowing scene is from the Bayeux tapestry. It was made more than 900 years ago, to tell the story of the Norman Conquest of England in 1066. The Normans (or "Northmen") were descended from a group of Vikings who had helped the king of France to defend his country from other Vikings. These Vikings were given land in France in 911. The Normans who invaded England were very different from their Viking ancestors, but their farming methods were very similar.

Spring was a busy time for everybody on a Viking farm if they were to have enough to eat for the following year. Before any crops could be planted, the fields had to be plowed. The children then removed any stones that the plow had brought to the surface. After this, the farmer sowed the seeds of barley, wheat, rye, or oats, which had been saved from the previous harvest. Once the seeds started to grow, the children were kept busy again. They pulled out

◁ Viking women spent a long time each day grinding grain on round stones called querns. They poured the grain through a hole in the top, then turned the top stone around and around with the handle. This squashed the grain between the two stones and eventually turned it into flour. Sometimes bits of the stone were ground in, too, and these wore down the Vikings' teeth when they were eating bread!

△ As well as mending their boats in winter, the Vikings used tools like these to make carts and sleds for moving things around on their farms. They made barrels, buckets, and other containers out of wood for storing food and drink. They probably also made furniture for their houses, but very little of it has survived.

the weeds and chased the birds away. At the same time, the vegetables were planted in the gardens and manure was spread on the hayfields to help the grass to grow.

As the weather became warmer, the sheep and cattle were taken away from the farm to summer pastures, or shielings. This meant that all the grass in the fields around the farm could be cut for hay in the early summer. After haymaking, there was a quiet time before the crops were ripe enough to harvest. This was when many of the men set out on raiding or trading adventures. The women ran the farms during this time.

The grain harvest in early autumn was a very busy time, and all the men tried to be back by then. Everyone helped to cut and harvest the crops and to take the grain back to the farmyard. Some of the grain was set aside to plant for the next year's crop. The rest was **threshed** to separate the hard seed cases, or **chaff**, from the grain. The grain was then stored until it was needed. It might be ground into flour or used for making beer.

As the weather turned cold again, the farmers had to decide how many animals they could feed over the winter. There was not enough hay to feed them all, so the weakest ones were killed to provide meat for the family.

Winters were long, dark, and cold in the Viking homelands. It was impossible to work out of doors. Winter was not an idle time, however. The men made and mended tools and kept the boats in good repair, while the women were kept busy spinning and weaving cloth, making clothes, and feeding their families.

▽ This wooden food container was found at a Viking farmhouse in Iceland. The owner carved a design on the lid.

△ Viking hunters would have looked very much like this Anglo-Saxon farmer. This scene is taken from a page in the calendar for September.

▽ Vikings in Iceland probably found whales like this one washed up on the shore. The whales provided meat and oil that could be used in lamps for lighting Viking homes.

Hunting and fishing

The Vikings who lived in the countryside went hunting and fishing. They trained falcons, hawks, and other birds to hunt and kill wild birds and small animals such as hares. The Vikings also trained dogs to bring back whatever the hawks killed. These dogs were highly valued. Strict rules were laid down about how much one hunter had to pay if he killed another Viking's dog. Other animals that the Vikings hunted included rabbits, deer, bears, and elks.

Most Vikings lived near the sea or beside rivers and lakes. Sometimes they fished from small boats, dangling a line with a **baited hook** on the end of it over the side. They also caught

Many remains of seeds have been found on various sites. They show that the Vikings gathered wild nuts, fruits, and berries. These included hazelnuts and walnuts, raspberries, strawberries, cherries, sloes, and elderberries.

The Vikings in Iceland collected seabirds' eggs from nests on the cliffs. This was done between mid-May and mid-June, which was known as "Egg-month." They also caught and ate birds such as puffins and guillemots.

"King Olaf rode out early with his hawks and dogs. When they let the hawks loose, the king's hawk killed two woodcocks in one flight. Then the hawk flew forward again and killed three more. The dogs followed them and caught every bird that fell to the ground."

A description of hunting taken from *St. Olaf's Saga*

▷ Fishing scenes were popular subjects for stone carvings in Viking times. Many carvings are connected with legends of the Viking gods and goddesses.

fish by spearing them in the shallow water near the shore. If they wanted to catch more than one fish at a time, the Vikings probably used a net.

Archaeologists have studied the remains of bones on Viking sites. The bones show that herring and cod were probably the favorite saltwater fish, while trout and salmon were popular freshwater fish. The remains of shells show that the Vikings also ate lots of shellfish, such as oysters.

▽ The Vikings used these to wind up their fishing lines.

Country feasts

The Vikings held three main feasts each year. These were Sigrblot in late spring or early summer, Vetrarblot in early autumn, and Jolablot in midwinter. The word *blot* means offering, or **sacrifice**. At each feast the Vikings were meant to sacrifice a horse to their gods.

As the Vikings were down-to-earth people who found horses useful on their farms, they often found ways of getting around this. One way was to sacrifice a very old horse that could no longer work. They then cooked its

Preserving food

Fish were kept, or **preserved**, by being smoked, salted, or dried in the sun. The last method was the easiest. The fish were **gutted** and opened out flat, then hung over a wooden rack in the open air. Salting was more difficult, as the salt itself had to be obtained by **evaporating** seawater to make salt crystals.

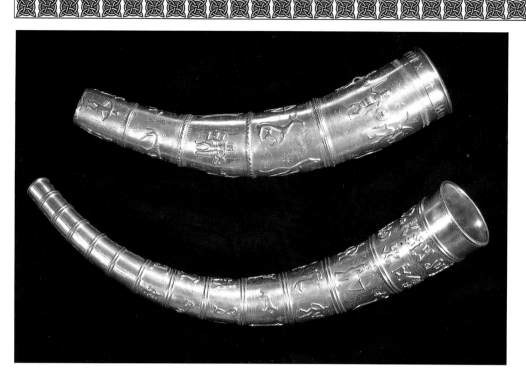

◁ At their feasts, the Vikings drank beer out of horns similar to these. A drinking horn could not stand on the table without spilling its contents. If a Viking could not empty the horn in one drink, he might pass it on to someone else.

meat and ate it at the feast. Sometimes the people made a bargain with the gods and goddesses, to share the horse with them. The horse then belonged to the Vikings while it was alive, but belonged to the gods when it died. In exchange for sacrifices, the Vikings asked their gods and goddesses for good harvests, victories in battles, and mild winters.

Each celebration lasted up to two weeks, especially in winter when it was cold and dark outside. As well as horsemeat, the Vikings ate beef, pork, veal, and mutton at their feasts. The meat might be roasted on a **spit**, or stewed in a **cauldron** over the fire, and was served up on wooden plates. There were no forks, but the Vikings had knives and spoons and they also used their fingers. There was plenty of beer and **mead** to drink, and the richest Vikings enjoyed wine.

The meals were eaten in the main hall of the longhouse. Tables were set out on the two long sides of the

▽ A cauldron from a Viking farm in Iceland.

The Vikings were expected to give their guests a warm welcome. *The Havamal* told them, "When a guest arrives chilled to the very knees from his journey, he needs fire, food and dry clothes."

central **hearth**. The host and hostess sat in the **high-seats** at the center of one table. Their guests sat next to them, in order of importance. After the meal, there was probably dancing and singing, as well as poetry reading and storytelling. When everyone was tired, the family went to their bedrooms, and the guests slept in the hall on beds made of blankets and animal skins.

△ This silver pendant from Sweden shows the clothes and hairstyle of a Viking woman.

 Thor was the favorite god of the Vikings. They believed that he was huge and jolly and had a red beard. He carried a hammer called Mjollnir, which he used to get himself out of trouble. Thor also liked to have fun. He is said to have stolen a cauldron of beer from the enemy giants, so that the gods and goddesses could have a party.

The Havamal

Odin was the wisest and most important of the Viking gods. He is supposed to have given the Vikings good advice. Some of this was later written down in a book called *The Havamal*. Some of this advice is about drinking, and includes the following:

"There is no better load a man can carry than much common sense—no worse a load than too much to drink. . . . Beer is not so good for a man as it is said to be. The more a man drinks, the less control he has of his thoughts."

◁ The remains of this Viking sword were found at Hedeby, Denmark.

Food in towns and cities

▷ This is the Viking market town of Birka in Sweden as it appears today. It was built on an island on Lake Mälaren, where waterways from the east and the south met. The water around Birka was very shallow, however, and the land it was built on was rising. Eventually, it became impossible for ships to reach the town. Birka was abandoned by the end of the Viking Age.

Living in a Viking town

Most Vikings lived in the country, but some towns did grow up around markets and trading centers. There the Vikings could buy and sell goods. The most important towns were Birka in Sweden, Hedeby in Denmark, and Kaupang in Norway.

Some Vikings who settled overseas also lived in towns. The most important Viking

Archaeologists excavated the Viking site at Coppergate in York in the 1970s. They found more than 30,000 objects that had been lost or thrown away by the people who had lived there. They also found evidence that showed that the Vikings suffered from fleas, head lice, and stomach worms!

◁ Many Vikings were skilled craftworkers. They made beautiful and practical items out of wood, metal, bone, antler, glass, and pottery. They also made dice and gaming pieces like these. Most items were produced in workshops behind the Vikings' houses. They were sold on stalls or booths in the street. Some traders bought goods to take overseas. They sold or exchanged them for other goods that the Vikings could not make.

towns in England were York, which they called Jorvik, and the Five Boroughs of Derby, Leicester, Lincoln, Nottingham, and Stamford.

In Ireland, Viking raiders started to build bases, or **long-phorts**. The first of these was Dublin, which began in 841. The others were Wexford, Cork, Waterford, and Limerick. They were planned as places where the raiders could stay over the winter. However, soon they began to attract traders, craftworkers, and **merchants** and to develop into towns.

The houses in Viking towns were often crammed tightly together and, as they were built mainly of wood, there was always a risk of fire. The streets were unpaved. There were no drains or flushing lavatories. Garbage was usually piled up in the streets or buried in pits behind the houses. The human waste went into a **cesspit**, which was often dug right next to the well that provided drinking water for the household!

△ Both hosts and guests wore their best clothes and jewelry when they went to a feast. For a woman, however, brooches were not only a way of showing off her wealth, but also a necessity for fastening her clothes. She usually had two oval brooches to fasten the straps of her tunic, and these often had a necklace between them. If it was cold, she also needed a third brooch to fasten her shawl in place.

▷ Viking men were proud of their appearance. They spent a lot of time using combs like these. In England, some of the Anglo-Saxons complained that the Vikings attracted all the women because they combed their hair, had baths, and changed their clothes so often!

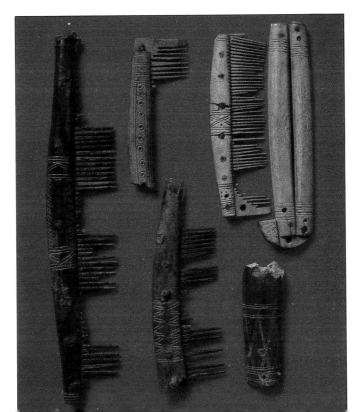

▽ When archaeologists excavate a site, they take samples of the soil back to their laboratories. There they try to find out more about the site in the past.

This soil is passed through sieves to separate out all the fragments of bones, shells, and seeds. These are then examined and identified, with the help of a powerful microscope.

These remains give us clues about what people ate in the past. They also tell us something about the plants and animals that lived on a particular site.

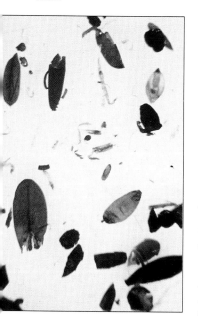

Obtaining food

Most houses in Viking towns were long and narrow. The narrow end of the house faced onto the street. Behind the house there was usually a workshop and a storeroom and, behind this, a small yard or garden. Many people kept a pig or two, for meat. Others kept a goat, which would provide them with milk to drink or to make into cheese or butter. The yard could also be used for growing vegetables such as carrots, parsnips, celery, peas, and beans. Herbs might also be grown there and perhaps an apple tree. Many people also kept hens and geese, but these were allowed to wander in the streets. They fed on the piles of rubbish and on the many weeds that grew there.

The grain crops were grown in fields outside the town, and the grain was brought in after it had been threshed. Nuts, fruits, and berries

△ A reconstruction of a town house at Jorvik that shows the kinds of food the Vikings ate and stored.

▷ This beautifully carved wooden cart belonged to a Viking queen. Simple wooden carts with wooden wheels were a common sight in the streets of a Viking town. They were used to take goods to and from ships at the docks and to bring in food and other items from the surrounding countryside.

were gathered from the countryside, to add variety to the Vikings' diet. Cattle and sheep were kept outside the town, too. They were brought into the town to be slaughtered and butchered when necessary.

Many Viking towns were built beside lakes or rivers or on the coast, and so fish was important to the people who lived there. Some of the fish was caught locally, but some was also brought in by ship from other areas. For example, barrels of salted herring were brought from Iceland to the quayside at Jorvik. They were exchanged for the grain that Iceland needed. The Vikings in Iceland could not grow enough crops, because the growing season there was shorter.

Cooking in towns

Most houses in Viking towns were smaller than those in the countryside. Often they had only one room, in which the entire family ate, slept, and kept all their belongings. This room was usually dark, even in the middle of the day, as the Vikings did not know how to make glass for windows. Some houses had holes cut into the walls to let in the light. These

▽ These portable scales were used by Viking traders. They weighed the pieces of silver, which were often used instead of coins to pay for goods.

▽ One of the luxuries that Vikings in towns could enjoy was high-quality wine. It was imported from the Rhineland of Germany in pottery jugs like this one.

▽ An iron spit that the Vikings used to roast meat over the fire

△ As this reconstruction from Jorvik shows, the inside of a Viking town house was very cluttered. The hearth was the center of all the activity.

Food was stored in wooden barrels and tubs against the walls, while herbs were hung from the rafters to dry. There is no evidence of cupboards or drawers in the houses. Cooking utensils were probably hung from nails on the walls. Spare pans, plates, bowls, and cups were probably kept on shelves until they were needed.

holes also let the drafts in, so they were closed with wooden shutters in cold weather. The main light then came from the fire, which burned in a hearth in the middle of the room. As there were no chimneys, the fire was open on all sides and its smoke had to escape through the roof.

The fire was used for cooking all the family's food. As in the country, grinding grain into flour and then baking it into bread were daily tasks for Viking women in towns. When the dough was ready, it was shaped into loaves. Then the loaves were placed on a flat stone slab across one end of the fire to bake. The bread became very hard and stale if it was not eaten within a day because it was baked without **yeast**.

Meat was roasted over the fire or stewed with vegetables in an iron pot or cauldron. The cauldrons were made from fairly thin metal, so

 This large earthenware jar was found in the Coppergate site in York. It may have held liquids such as **buttermilk**, which the Vikings drank in large quantities.

holes were burned in them if they stood over the flames for too long. To avoid this, the Vikings often heated small stones in the fire and then dropped them into cold water in the cauldron. This helped to heat the water so that it took less time to boil once the cauldron was put over the fire. When the water was hot enough, joints of pork or ham could be put in to boil. Some meat and fish were also baked or grilled in the **embers** when the fire burned low.

▽ The Vikings had to keep their fires lit nearly all the time, for heating and cooking. They needed a large supply of firewood, which they gathered from nearby woods and forests.

There was nowhere in a Viking town where people could go out for a meal. All the food had to be cooked at home.

▷ Jarls in Iceland held open-air meetings every year here at Thingvellir.

The sagas tell us that the Vikings played harps and fiddles. They also danced to the sound of singing. However, one Arab trader who visited the Viking town of Hedeby wrote, "I have never heard a more horrible singing. It is like a growl coming out of their throats, like dogs barking, only much more beastly."

In this description from *The Saga of the Men of Keelness*, a Viking from Iceland, called Bui, is being given a meal by Frith, the daughter of a king. "She drew up a fair table and laid it. Then she carried [to Bui] a silver basin and a costly towel, and afterward asked him to eat and drink. She fetched in delicious food and splendid drink. All of the table things, dishes, goblets, and spoons, were of silver decorated with gold. Frith sat down by Bui, and they ate and drank together."

A royal feast

Before the Vikings were ruled by kings, each jarl had his own group of followers among the local karls. As the population grew, people began living closer to one another. One jarl would then become more powerful than the others in an area. He might even be known as a king, but he was king only in his own area. He did not rule the whole country.

Laws were set and disputes were settled at open-air meetings of all the karls in an area. These meetings were called Things and each

◁ A gold or silver bracelet made an ideal gift for a traveling poet, or skald. If he did not want to wear it, he might exchange it with a merchant or trader for something of equal value. He might also cut it up into small pieces that could be weighed out and used like coins to buy other goods.

hIC FECERVN: PRANDIVM:
ET hIC EPISCOPVS:CIBV:ET
POTV: BE NE DIC IT.

△ There are no surviving pictures that show a Viking royal feast. Descriptions in the sagas tell us that it would probably have looked like this one, from the Bayeux tapestry.

one had its own set of laws. Even when kings ruled in Denmark, Norway, and Sweden, the Things still dealt with local matters. These included land ownership, theft, and divorce. They also had the power to make someone an outlaw, or **nithing**, and to send him away, into exile.

Both jarls and kings liked to entertain people on a lavish scale. They gave their guests plenty to eat and drink, but in return they expected generous gifts, as well as loyalty. The gifts included jewelry, which was worn both by men and women, weapons, and even fully equipped longships.

Food at a royal feast was probably very similar to that at a country feast. There was plenty of meat, fish, and cheese to eat, and beer, mead, and wine to drink. Servants brought food and drink to the tables and made sure that all the guests had as much as they wanted. After the meal, a skald would start to recite poetry. Some of it was recited from memory, but the most important part was the poem, the *drapa*, which he made up on the spot in praise of his host. If the host was pleased with the *drapa*, he gave the skald a valuable gift.

▽ As well as glassware, a king might have silver wine cups for good-quality wine on his table. He would also have silver dishes. In spite of this, he and his guests picked their food up in their fingers or scooped it up on a piece of bread. There were no forks.

Food for travelers

Viking adventurers

The Vikings made careful preparations before setting out on a long sea journey. They made sure that their ship and all its equipment were in good condition, and they stocked up with plenty of food and water. The food included cheese and butter and salted and smoked fish and meat. It probably also included apples and nuts and whatever vegetables were in season. Everything was packed into wooden tubs and barrels and stored under the half decks at each end of the ship. A large iron cauldron and its three-legged stand, or tripod, were also put on board for cooking.

Whenever possible, the Vikings sailed close to the coast. This meant that they could come ashore at night and light a fire to cook. If they were too far from the coast to do this, they might have made a fire in a strongbox. The box

When Leif Eriksson sailed from Greenland to look for North America, he went first to Baffin Island, then to Labrador, and to Newfoundland. Leif called the last place he visited Vinland. This may be because he used the wild berries growing there to make wine.

▽ This map shows the main routes used by the Vikings. Those who went to the east sailed down the rivers. From the trading center at Ladoga they could follow the Volga River and cross the Caspian Sea. They then left their ships and went by camel to Baghdad, where they traded for silks, spices, and silver.

Other Vikings went south from Ladoga to Novgorod and then along the Dnieper River. To get there, they had to lift their ships out of the water and transport them overland for some distance. They then sailed down to Kiev and across the Black Sea to trade in Istanbul, which they called Miklagaard.

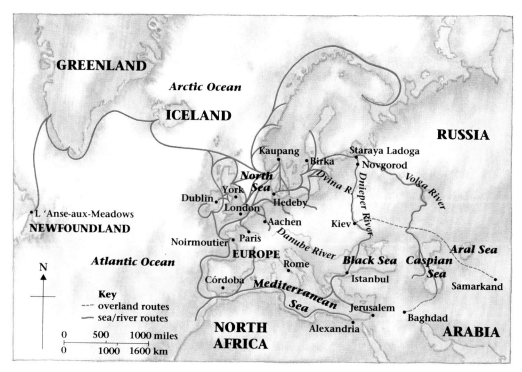

△ Viking traders brought good-quality glassware from the Rhineland. It was probably very expensive. Only wealthy people such as kings, jarls, and merchants could afford to buy it.

was filled with sand to stop the flames from spreading.

The Vikings had no maps or charts. They passed on instructions for sailing from one place to another by word of mouth. Some of these instructions were later written down. One of them tells how to get from Norway to Greenland. "From Hernar in Norway set sail due west for Hvarf in Greenland. Sail to the north of Shetland so that you can just sight it in clear weather, but to the south of the Faeroes so that the sea seems to be halfway up the mountain slopes, and steer south of Iceland in such a way that you can sight birds and whales from there."

△ This Viking ship was discovered at Gokstad in Norway. It had been buried under a mound of clay. The clay stopped the air from getting to the wood and rotting it. Archaeologists have restored it so that we can see how it looked in Viking times.

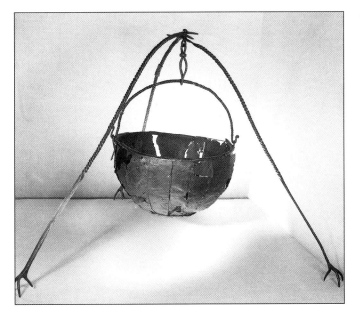

◁ Viking travelers cooked with a cauldron like this one. The tripod held the cauldron clear of the flames so that the bottom of it did not burn through.

The journey to Valhalla

The Vikings believed that their final journey took place after they had died. They thought they went on to an **afterlife** which was very much like this one—but it lasted forever.

Warriors believed that if they died in battle, they would go straight to Valhalla. This was the home of Odin, who was the god of warriors and noblemen. When they arrived, their wounds would be healed and they would be brought back to life. They could fight all day against one another, then come back to Odin's hall and feast all night, before going out to fight again the next day. Viking warriors who died in their beds, however, could not go to Valhalla. Instead, they went to a place called Niflheim. This was underneath the earth and was full of ice and mist.

To help the Vikings on their journey to the afterlife, food, drink, and cooking equipment were buried along with them. Wealthy Vikings were buried in ships to take them on the journey.

One of these ships was discovered at Oseberg in Norway in 1904. It was the grave of a royal lady. She had been buried with an elderly servant who would do all the cooking for her on the journey to the afterlife. The remains of some of the food were also found on board the ship. There were two oxen, wheat, oats, wild apples, hazelnuts, cress, horseradish, and mustard.

△ This statue is of the god Odin. He was said to be very wise, because he had given one of his eyes in exchange for the gift of knowledge. Odin rode around Valhalla on an eight-legged horse called Sleipnir. He had two pet ravens called Hugin and Munin, who helped him to know about everything that was going on in the world.

▽ This stone carving from Gotland in Sweden shows a Viking arriving in Valhalla. He is being greeted by one of Odin's maidens, or Valkyries. She is offering him a drink in a drinking horn.

◁ This is some of the kitchen equipment that was found on board the Oseberg ship. There was also an iron cauldron with a chain and a tripod to hang it from. A collection of spades, a hoe, and a manure fork were provided, to help with the growing of more food in the afterlife!

An Arab called Ibn Fadlan witnessed a Viking **cremation** on the banks of the Volga River in 922. He left a full description of the event.

The man who had died was dressed in his best clothes and then placed in a tent on board his ship. There was food and drink in the tent for him, including the meat of two horses, two cows, a hen, and a cockerel. The ship was then set on fire and when the flames died down, all the ashes were gathered up and placed in a memorial mound.

▷ Over the years many Vikings became Christians, which made it easier for them to trade with Christians in other lands. However, they often worshiped their own gods as well. Molds like this one were used to make Thor's hammers or Christian crosses. When the Vikings became Christians, they no longer put food and other items in their graves.

Meals and recipes

The Vikings usually ate two main meals a day. They ate the first one at about eight o'clock in the morning and the other at about seven o'clock at night. In between they probably also had a snack of bread and cheese if they were hungry.

They ate a lot of dairy produce and were especially fond of buttermilk, which is a thick, sour milk. They also used whey, the part of the milk left over from cheese making, to preserve some of their food. The Vikings had no potatoes, rice, or pasta and so they ate a great deal of bread. Many Vikings kept bees and used their honey to sweeten food, as well as for making mead. There was no sugar. Fish was often dried or salted and transported over long distances, but meat and vegetables had to be produced locally.

The meat of animals that were killed in the autumn was preserved for the winter by salting, smoking, or drying. By the end of the winter, however, it often began to taste bad. Herbs such as garlic were used to try to hide the taste.

Fresh meat and fresh fish were often grilled on an open fire, rather like cooking food on a barbecue today. The Vikings sometimes also cooked fish between two layers of grass, with red-hot stones underneath and on top. Today we would probably wrap the fish up in aluminium foil and put it in the oven to bake.

Recipes

Although no Viking recipes exist, the sagas and the archaeological evidence tell us that they would have used recipes very much like these. Ask an adult for help when you plan the meals and start to prepare the food.

> **WARNING:** Sharp knives and boiling liquids are dangerous. Hot ovens and pans can burn you. *Always ask an adult to help you* when you are preparing or cooking food in the kitchen.

Porridge

Ingredients

2¹/₂ cups water

a pinch of salt

¹/₄ cup oatmeal

milk and honey, to
serve

**Ask an adult to
help you when you
start to cook.**

1. Measure out the water and put it into the
   saucepan. Bring it to a boil.
2. Add the salt to the boiling water.
3. Measure the oatmeal. Add the oatmeal to the
   water very gradually, stirring it well with a
   wooden spoon.
4. Let the mixture boil again.
5. Boil gently for 20 minutes if the oatmeal is
   fine, or for 30 minutes if the oatmeal is coarse.
6. Pour the porridge into the bowls. Add cold
   milk and honey to taste.

Equipment

measuring cup

saucepan

wooden spoon

two bowls

Hot liquids and pans
are dangerous.

Parsley butter

Ingredients

3T freshly chopped
parsley

¹/₂ cup butter

black pepper

Sharp knives and hot
pans are dangerous.

1. Carefully chop the parsley very finely. Take
   care to keep your fingers away from the blade
   of the knife.
2. Let the butter soften at room temperature.
3. Put the softened butter into a mixing bowl
   with a wooden spoon and add the chopped
   parsley and black pepper. Mix everything
   together very well.
4. Shape the mixture into a block. Wrap the block
   in foil and put it in the refrigerator to cool.
5. Cut slices of parsley butter from the block and
   serve with any broiled fish, such as salmon.

Equipment

sharp knife

chopping board

measuring cup

wooden spoon

mixing bowl

aluminium foil

Broiled salmon

Ingredients

(for each person)

1 salmon steak

2T butter

salt

**Ask an adult to
help you when you
start to cook.**

1. Line the broiler pan with foil. This will catch
   any butter or other liquid dripping off the fish
   and make washing up easier afterward!
2. Place the salmon steaks in the colander and
   wash them in cold running water.
3. Dry the salmon steaks with paper towels and
   place them on the broiler pan.
4. Put the butter into a small saucepan on a very
   low heat. Remove the saucepan from the heat
   when the butter has melted.

Equipment

aluminium foil

colander

paper towels

measuring cup

small saucepan

brush for butter

serving dish

5. Brush the salmon steaks generously with the melted butter, and then sprinkle a little salt over them.
6. Put the salmon steaks under a heated broiler and cook for six to eight minutes on each side. (Ask an adult to help you turn the fish.)
7. When the salmon steaks are cooked through, carefully remove them from the broiler and put them on the serving dish.
8. If you wish, put slices of parsley butter on the salmon steaks, and serve immediately.

Pork and leek stew

Ingredients

1 lb lean boneless pork

3–4 short pieces of marrow bone

5 cups water

2 leeks

3 carrots

1 onion

2 stalks of celery

1 tsp dried sage or dried mixed herbs

2T fine oatmeal

salt

Equipment

sharp knife

chopping board

large saucepan

wooden spoon

slotted spoon

measuring cup

serving dish

Ask an adult to help you when you start to cook.

Hot liquids, hot pans, and sharp knives are dangerous.

1. Ask an adult to chop the meat into two-inch cubes.
2. Put the chopped meat, marrow bones, and water into a large saucepan and bring to a boil.
3. When the liquid is boiling, ask an adult to skim the floating fat from the surface.
4. Turn the heat down and cover the pan with a lid. Let the meat and bones simmer in the liquid for about two hours.
5. While the meat is cooking, wash and clean the leeks thoroughly. Carefully chop the leeks into small rings, taking care to keep your fingers away from the blade of the knife.
6. Clean the carrots and chop them into small pieces, taking care not to cut your fingers.
7. Carefully remove the peel from the onion. Cut the onion in half, and then slice each half thinly. Be careful of your fingers!
8. Cut out any bad parts of the celery and throw them away. Wash the celery and chop into small pieces.
9. When the meat is almost cooked, remove the marrow bones with a slotted spoon. Then add the chopped vegetables and the sage or mixed herbs.
10. Let the stew simmer for a further 15 to 20 minutes until the vegetables are soft. Ask an adult to skim any fat from the surface of the stew.

11. Stir in the oatmeal. Then turn the heat up again to bring the stew back to a boil.
12. Cook the stew for a further 10 minutes and add salt to taste.
13. Pour the stew into a serving dish.

Baked trout stuffed with onions and mushrooms

Ingredients

1 medium-sized trout
1 small onion
$1/4$ cup mushrooms
1T freshly chopped parsley
2T butter

Ask an adult to help you when you start to cook.

Equipment

colander
chopping board
sharp knife
measuring cup
skillet
wooden spoon
aluminium foil
spatula
serving dish

Sharp knives and hot ovens are dangerous.

1. Put the fish in a colander and wash it thoroughly inside and outside in cold running water. Then leave it in the colander to dry.
2. Ask an adult to set the oven to 375°F.
3. Peel the onion and chop it into small pieces with a sharp knife. Take care to keep your fingers away from the knife blade.
4. Clean the mushrooms and peel them. Carefully cut them into thin slices, using a sharp knife.
5. Carefully chop the parsley very finely, using a sharp knife.
6. Measure the butter and then melt it in the skillet, over a low heat.
7. Mix the chopped onion with the melted butter using a wooden spoon. Stir the mixture until the onion starts to change color. Then add the mushrooms.
8. Stir the mushroom and onion mixture until it is soft. Take the skillet off the heat and stir in the chopped parsley.
9. Tear off a piece of foil large enough to wrap up the trout. Lay the foil flat and put the fish in the middle of it. Use the wooden spoon to stuff the inside of the trout with the onion and mushroom mixture.
10. Fold the foil around the fish so that it is wrapped up in a parcel.
11. Ask an adult to put the fish in the oven for you. Let the fish bake for 15 to 20 minutes. Then ask an adult to take the parcel out of the oven.
12. Open the parcel very carefully (hot steam will come out). Use a spatula to lift the fish onto the serving dish and serve immediately.

Glossary

afterlife:	Another life, very much like this one, which the Vikings believed they would enjoy after they died.
ancestors:	People from whom one is directly descended; for example, a grandmother or great-grandfather.
archaeologist:	Someone who finds out about life in the past by looking for and carefully studying objects from earlier times. These objects include seeds and bones, as well as items made by people.
baited hook:	A fishing hook with food such as a worm fixed on to attract the fish.
buttermilk:	The liquid left over after the cream has been removed from the milk to make butter.
cauldron:	A large metal pan for boiling or stewing food over an open fire.
cereal crops:	Crops such as wheat, barley, rye, and oats that have grain, or "ears." The name comes from the Roman goddess of the harvest, Ceres.
cesspit:	A hole in the ground, used as a lavatory. It was very unhygienic as there was no way of flushing the waste away.
chaff:	The hard, brittle shell that protects grain seeds as they are growing.
cremation:	The act of burning the body of a dead person.
dairy produce:	Food such as cheese, butter, and cream, all made from milk.
embers:	The hot glowing part left in the bottom of a fire when the flames die down.
evaporate:	To turn from liquid into vapor. In the case of saltwater, crystals of salt were left behind after the water evaporated.
excavate:	To dig up objects from the past in a scientific manner, to find out more about how people lived in that place in earlier times.
gutting:	Removing the insides of an animal or fish before cooking.
hearth:	A place made for a fire to burn safely, so that it does not spread and set the building on fire.
high-seat:	The seat belonging to the owner of a Viking longhouse. It had carved posts on either side of it and was always placed nearest to the fire.
longhouse:	A Viking farmhouse. It was long and narrow in shape.
long-phort:	One of the places in Ireland where the Vikings first stayed for the winter. The long-phorts later developed into trading towns.
longships:	The long, narrow ships used by the Vikings on their raiding expeditions.
manure:	The waste from animals, which was gathered in the farmyard over the winter and spread on the fields in spring to enrich the soil.
mead:	A sweet alcoholic drink made with honey.
merchant:	Someone who makes a living by buying and selling goods.

monastery:	A place where monks live and practice their religion.
monk:	A man who has devoted his life to God and who lives with other monks in a monastery.
***nithing*:**	Someone who would not accept the law of the Thing. He then became an outlaw and had to leave the district as anyone could then kill him without fear of punishment.
preserve:	To treat food so that it can be kept for some time without going bad.
runes:	The marks or letters used to write down the Viking language. They were made up of straight lines that were easy to carve on stone, metal, or wood.
sacrifice:	An offering made by people to please their gods. It often involved the killing of an animal, but also could be the giving up of a favorite possession.
saga:	One of the long stories of the Viking adventures. The sagas were first written down in Iceland during the 13th century.
scythe:	A long-handled tool with a long, sharp blade. It was used to cut grass.
sickle:	A tool with a short handle and a curved blade. It was used to cut crops.
smithy:	The place where a blacksmith works. It has a very hot fire, or forge, on which to heat bars of iron to make or mend tools and other items.
spit:	A long thin metal bar, often pointed at one end, on which food is fixed to be cooked.
thatch:	To use a thick layer of material such as straw, reeds or heather to make a roof.
thresh:	To remove the chaff from the grain by beating it with sticks, or flails.
yeast:	A type of fungus that is used in baking to make bread light and soft.

Further reading

Ganeri, Anita. *Focus on Vikings*. New York: Franklin Watts, 1992.

Humble, Richard. *The Age of Leif Eriksson*. New York: Franklin Watts, 1989.

Martell, Hazel Mary. *The Vikings (Worlds of the Past)*. New York: New Discovery Books, 1991.

———. *Over 900 Years Ago: With the Vikings*. New York: New Discovery Books, 1993.

———. *The Vikings and Jorvik*. New York: Dillon Books, 1993.

Mulvihill, Margaret. *Viking Longboats*. New York: Franklin Watts, 1989.

Index